Hurrell's Hollywood

Photographs by George Hurrell
A Book of Postcards

Pomegranate Artbooks, San Francisco

Pomegranate Artbooks
Box 808022
Petaluma, CA 94975

ISBN 0-87654-750-1
Pomegranate Catalog Number A569

Pomegranate publishes several other postcard collections on many different subjects.
Please write to the publisher for more information.

Cover design by Patty Burke

*T*HE HURRELL STYLE is immediately identifiable.

George Hurrell, one of America's greatest celebrity photographers, immortalized the silver screen's legendary stars of the '20s, '30s and '40s. His career continued into the 1990s. In sleek, dramatically-lit and always glamorous poses, Hurrell's method signified a new photographic style, *The Hurrell Style*, which influenced generations of fashion and portrait photographers. Hurrell's ageless images elevated his subjects to icons of beauty, youth and sex appeal.

His work was markedly different from that of his Hollywood predecessors and peers Ruth Harriet Louise and Edwin Bower Hesser, among others. In the late 1920s, most studio publicity shots were soft-focus idealizations, pictures of perfection, primped and printed to obliterate even the most insignificant (but often endearing) flaw or hint of human character. Hurrell was both more sensitive and more ruthless than that. His mature work reveals a precise instinct for the key, climatic event of a photo session. His visual alertness, his insight and the exercise of his perception echo the shrewdness of Edward Weston's portraits.

Born in 1904 in Cincinnati, Ohio, Hurrell moved to Los Angeles in the early '20s to study painting and photography. He opened his own studio in 1927 and with his first star portrait of Ramon Novarro launched a long, successful career. From the 1920s through the '40s he photographed all the major stars working for the big studios, MGM, Warner Brothers and Columbia in particular. He transformed Norma Shearer's public image of the "girl next door" into that of an alluring seductress, giving her a "look" that garnered her Oscar-winning role in *The Divorcee* (1930).

Hurrell understood our need for illusion and generously fed the hunger. His publicity photos were an important element in the image-creation industry that gave America its own gods and goddesses: movie stars. He photographed flesh as if it were marble, with light the chisel. When capturing glamor, he painstakingly maintained the distance between viewer and subject; the stars remained as far away as the ones in the sky, a key element in the magic. Hurrell exploited such magic for all its worth.

In his active later years, intense and direct as he was seemingly imperious, George Hurrell clearly knew his subjects as well as he understood the magic he created with his camera. "If you don't have any beauty inside, you can't have any beauty outside. You just have a false face that is well designed. That's all."

But he scoffed at reference to any magic in his method. "Usually it just takes a couch or some other background and a sense of composition, a pose. The rest is lighting. Lighting can change personality completely. I always had an understanding about lighting."

The pictures in this book have been reproduced in rich duotone to re-create the warm subtle tints which suffuse the originals. The photographs were printed by George Hurrell.

"A Hurrell portrait is to the ordinary publicity still what a Rolls Royce is to a roller skate."
    Esquire magazine, 1936

Hurrell's Hollywood

Ramon Novarro (Mexican, 1899–1968). Exotic and romantic leading man of the '20s, he later came back as a character actor. His best films include *Ben Hur* (1925) and *Call of the Flesh* (1930).

Pomegranate • Box 808022 • Petaluma, CA 94975

Hurrell's Hollywood

Judy Garland (American, 1922–69). Hollywood made her into
one of its all-time immortals and burned her up in the
process. Her name will always be closely linked to Dorothy
and the *Wizard of Oz* (1939).

Pomegranate • Box 808022 • Petaluma, CA 94975

Hurrell's Hollywood

Greta Garbo (Swedish, 1905–90) A leading actress in Sweden when director Mauritz Stiller took her to Hollywood where she became the major myth figure in the history of film, best remembered for *Anna Karenina* (1933), *Camille* (1936) and *Ninotchka* (1939).

Pomegranate • Box 808022 • Petaluma, CA 94975

Hurrell's Hollywood

Hedy Lamarr (Austrian, b. 1913). After a sensational film
debut, a 10–minute nude gambol in the 1933 Czech production
Extase/Ecstasy, she came to Hollywood and appeared in
Algiers (1938) and *Samson and Delilah* (1949).

Pomegranate • Box 808022 • Petaluma, CA 94975

Hurrell's Hollywood

Norma Shearer (American, 1900–83). Sophisticated leading lady, her films include an Oscar-winning role in *The Divorcee* (1930), and *The Barretts of Wimpole Street* (1934).

Pomegranate • Box 808022 • Petaluma, CA 94975

Hurrell's Hollywood

Robert Taylor (American, 1911–69) The last of the matinée
idols, he appeared in *Magnificent Obsession* (1935) and *Quo
Vadis* (1951).

Pomegranate • Box 808022 • Petaluma, CA 94975

Hurrell's Hollywood

Bette Davis (American, 1908–89) Dramatic film star in
pictures *Jezebel* (1938) and *All About Eve* (1950), she later
played eccentric roles in *Whatever Happened to Baby Jane?*
(1962) and *Hush, Hush, Sweet Charlotte* (1964).

Pomegranate • Box 808022 • Petaluma, CA 94975

Hurrell's Hollywood

Joan Crawford (American, 1906–77) One of Hollywood's most
durable stars, she appeared in films such as *Mildred Pierce*
(1945) and *Whatever Happened to Baby Jane?* (1962).

Pomegranate • Box 808022 • Petaluma, CA 94975

Hurrell's Hollywood

Katharine Hepburn (American, b. 1907) A steadfast and
feisty actor whose determination has kept her active in film all
her adult life. Among her best performances are *Bringing Up
Baby* (1938) and *On Golden Pond* (1981).

Pomegranate • Box 808022 • Petaluma, CA 94975

Hurrell's Hollywood

Buster Keaton (American, 1895–1966) One of the finest early
film comedians and directors, his best include *Cops* (1922),
The General (1927), *The Cameraman* (1928) and *Sherlock
Junior* (1924).

Pomegranate • Box 808022 • Petaluma, CA 94975

Hurrell's Hollywood

James Cagney (American, 1899–1986). Classic film gangster and tough guy in movies like *The Public Enemy* (1931), he later won an Oscar as a song-and-dance man in *Yankee Doodle Dandy* (1941).

Pomegranate • Box 808022 • Petaluma, CA 94975

Hurrell's Hollywood

Barbara Stanwyck (American, 1907–90) Cast as the gutsy,
independent woman, hard-boiled on the outside, tender on the
inside, her movies include *Baby Face* (1933) and *Meet John
Doe* (1941).

Pomegranate • Box 808022 • Petaluma, CA 94975

Hurrell's Hollywood

Jean Harlow (American, 1911–37) Wisecracking, slatternly
and sexually voracious, she gave as good as she got. A great
film comedian still enjoyable today, her best films include
Hell's Angels (1930) and *Bombshell* (1933).

Pomegranate • Box 808022 • Petaluma, CA 94975

Hurrell's Hollywood

Humphrey Bogart (American, 1899–1957). Classic movie tough guy, a list of his many great films includes *Casablanca* (1942) and *African Queen* (1952).

Pomegranate • Box 808022 • Petaluma, CA 94975

Hurrell's Hollywood

Johnny Weissmuller (American, 1904–84) Olympic swimmer
who played Tarzan on film more than any other actor, starting
in 1932.

Pomegranate • Box 808022 • Petaluma, CA 94975

Hurrell's Hollywood

Gilbert Roland (Mexican, b. 1905) Trained as a bullfighter, he
gatecrashed Hollywood in the mid-twenties and was a popular
film star well into the 1970s.

Pomegranate • Box 808022 • Petaluma, CA 94975

Hurrell's Hollywood

William Powell (American, 1892–1984) Mature, debonair
leading man best remembered as Nick Charles in *The Thin
Man* (1934). Some of his other notable performances include
Life With Father (1947) and 'Doc' in *Mister Roberts* (1955).

Pomegranate • Box 808022 • Petaluma, CA 94975

Hurrell's Hollywood

Myrna Loy (American, b. 1905) Likeable 1930s "Queen of Hollywood," her films include *The Thin Man* (1934), *Libeled Lady* (1936) and *Cheaper by the Dozen* (1950).

Pomegranate • Box 808022 • Petaluma, CA 94975

Hurrell's Hollywood

Spencer Tracy (American, 1900–67) He began by playing thugs, grew into pals and priests, and became the epitome of the gruff, ethical American in films such as *Father of the Bride* (1950) and *Inherit the Wind* (1960).

Pomegranate • Box 808022 • Petaluma, CA 94975

Hurrell's Hollywood

Douglas Fairbanks, Jr. (American, b. 1909) Identified with
British upper crust characters, he also revived the swashbuck-
ling roles his father made famous in silent films. His films
include *Gunga Din* (1939) and *The Corsican Brothers* (1942).

Pomegranate • Box 808022 • Petaluma, CA 94975

Hurrell's Hollywood

Rita Hayworth (American, 1918–87) Leading lady and dancer as well as a leading WWII pin up, her films included *Gilda* (1946) and *Pal Joey* (1957).

Pomegranate • Box 808022 • Petaluma, CA 94975

Hurrell's Hollywood

Susan Hayward (American, 1918–75) Former model, the husky-voiced redhead specialized in fallen-women-fighting-back roles in docu–dramas such as *I'll Cry Tomorrow* (1956) and *I Want to Live* (1958), for which she won an Oscar.

Pomegranate • Box 808022 • Petaluma, CA 94975

Hurrell's Hollywood

Lionel Barrymore (American, 1878–1954) Celebrated
character actor played sentimental grandpas and churlish
millionaires in films including *Grand Hotel* (1932) and *It's a
Wonderful Life* (1946).

Pomegranate • Box 808022 • Petaluma, CA 94975

Hurrell's Hollywood

John Gilbert (American, 1895–1936) The undisputed king of silent screen romance after the death of Valentino in 1926, his best films include *Flesh and the Devil* (1927) and *Queen Christina* (1933) with his off-screen squeeze Greta Garbo.

Pomegranate • Box 808022 • Petaluma, CA 94975

Hurrell's Hollywood

Ann Sheridan (American, 1915–67) A cheerful beauty contest
winner who developed a tough style and became known as the
"oomph" girl, she starred in *They Drive by Night* (1940) and
I Was a Male War Bride (1949).

Pomegranate • Box 808022 • Petaluma, CA 94975

Hurrell's Hollywood

Laurence Olivier (English, 1907–89) A memorable
Shakespearean, an actor and director of stage and film,
called one of the most versatile and exciting performers in the
world, the actor's actor, his movies include *The Entertainer*
(1960), and *Sleuth* (1972).

Pomegranate • Box 808022 • Petaluma, CA 94975

Hurrell's Hollywood

Errol Flynn (Tasmanian, 1909–59) He led an adventurous life
on and off the screen. His handsome impudence was featured
in films such as *Captain Blood* (1935) and *The Adventures of
Robin Hood* (1938).

Pomegranate • Box 808022 • Petaluma, CA 94975

Hurrell's Hollywood

Ronald Coleman (English, 1891–1958) A distinguished
romantic actor of gentle manners, intelligence and good looks,
he appeared in *A Tale of Two Cities* (1935) and *Lost Horizon*
(1937) among other leading roles.

Pomegranate • Box 808022 • Petaluma, CA 94975

Hurrell's Hollywood

Robert Montgomery (American, 1904–81) Smooth, smart
leading man of '30s, he later turned to directing, television,
and then politics. His best films include *Night Must Fall* (1937)
and *Here Comes Mr. Jordan* (1941).

Pomegranate • Box 808022 • Petaluma, CA 94975

Hurrell's Hollywood

Tallulah Bankhead (American, 1902–68) Stage and screen
star noted for extravagant gestures and a gravel voice, she
appeared in *Lifeboat* (1943) and *A Royal Scandal* (1945).

Pomegranate • Box 808022 • Petaluma, CA 94975